Guitar Styles
from Around the Globe

Cuba
Your passport to a new world of music

MW00998957

JEFF PERETZ

Alfred Music Publishing Co., Inc.
16320 Roscoe Blvd., Suite 100
P.O. Box 10003
Van Nuys, CA 91410-0003
alfred.com

ISBN-10: 0-7390-4301-3
ISBN-13: 978-0-7390-4301-1

CD recorded by Steve Rossiter at Axis Sound, NYC
Jeff Peretz, guitar; Tony de Vivo, percussion and bass
Interior illustrations by Barbara Smolover
Cover photographs: © Brunomedley | Dreamstime.com
Guitar courtesy of Taylor Guitars.

Contents

0

Track 1

A compact disc is included with this book. This disc can make learning with the book easier and more enjoyable. The symbol shown at the left appears next to every example that is on the CD. Use the CD to help ensure that you're capturing the feel of the examples, interpreting the rhythms correctly, and so on. The track number below the symbol corresponds directly to the example you want to hear. Track 1 will help you tune your guitar to this CD.

Have fun!

About the Author

Jeff Peretz was born in Newark, New Jersey. He studied music at Berklee College of Music and William Paterson University, with a focus on jazz performance. He is the author of *Zen and the Art of Guitar* (Alfred/National Guitar Workshop #21906) and *Guitar Atlas: Middle East* (Alfred/National Guitar Workshop #22711). He can be heard regularly with the Arabic/Jazz group Abu Gara, which he founded in 1999. Jeff has performed all over the United States, the Middle East, and Europe. While his main instrument is the guitar, he regularly performs on ud and dumbek as well. He has played ud with Grammy-nominated Latin group Yerba Buena. His jazz/hip-hop group, the Jeff Peretz Group, has shared the stage with the Fugees, Groove Collective, and Brooklyn Funk Essentials. He is the director of the electric guitar performance program at the Third Street Music School Settlement in New York City and is a faculty member at The New School and New York University. He also teaches at the National Guitar Workshop.

PHOTO BY NETA KATZ

Acknowledgements

This book is dedicated to my beautiful children Maya, Tristen, and Zohar. Everything I do is for you three. Thanks to Ben Lapidus and Julian Kleinerman for their patience with all of my questions. Extra special gratitude to Tony de Vivo for "killin' it" in the session and Steve Rossiter for pressing all the right buttons as usual.

AUTHOR'S FOREWORD

What is it about the music of Cuba that has caused such a great impact in the world music genre? This question can be answered in many different ways, but for me, a total rhythm junkie, the answer is quite simple: rhythm. Nowhere else in the Western world do African rhythms and European harmonies come together with such toe-tapping, hip-shaking intensity. This book is a compilation of exercises, historical facts, and general bits of wisdom I have picked up through many years of playing and listening to Cuban music. I hope to demonstrate that the guitar (along with its cousin the *tres*) plays an important role in the multi-layered rhythmic quilt of Cuban music.

To benefit from this book, you should be comfortable reading either standard music notation or TAB. Understanding the theory behind major scales and chords will help you make sense of the exercises. If you need a refresher, you can refer to *Theory for the Contemporary Guitarist* by Guy Capuzzo (Alfred/National Guitar Workshop #16755). Cuban guitar playing requires many of the same skills as jazz guitar, which you can learn more about in *Beginning Jazz Guitar* (Alfred/National Guitar Workshop #14120) or *The Total Jazz Guitarist* (Alfred/National Guitar Workshop #24417). The accompanying CD will help you interpret the rhythm and feel of each example. Before we delve into the power of Cuban rhythm, however, let's begin by exploring the cultural influences that have shaped Cuban music.

Chapter 1 — HISTORY OF CUBAN MUSIC

Havana
CUBA

THE GOLDEN AGE

In 1940, after overthrowing the progressive government of Ramón Grau San Martin, Colonel Fulgencio Batista was elected to a four-year term as President of Cuba. In 1952, he overthrew the democratic government of Carlos Prío Socarrás to once again assume leadership. During his time in power, Batista courted investors and tourists from the United States. While this led to many mafia acquisitions of hotels, casinos, and mansions in and around Havana, it also led to an era of nightlife unlike any before. Despite the growing corruption of the Batista regime, music, dancing, and singing flourished in Havana in the 1950s. It was during this time that the music of Cuba became a major artistic force and established itself as a source of pride and identity for this island in the Caribbean. The 1950s are considered to be the golden era of Cuban music and nightlife.

The instability of the government didn't end with Batista. On December 31, 1958, Batista was ousted by Fidel Castro and his *barbudos* (bearded guerillas), including the revolutionary legend Ernesto "Che" Guevara. Despite the violence and fear that gripped the nation during these transitional times, the music and nightlife continued to attract people from all over the world. Legendary night spots like the Casino de la Playa and the Tropicana offered musical revues starring such celebrated performers as Celia Cruz (the "Godmother of Salsa"), Arsenio Rodríguez, Xiomara Alfaro, and the Valdés Brothers.

The excitement of the scene was not limited to the big night clubs and casinos. Small cafés such as El Paris and La Bombilla hosted local jam sessions known as *descargas* (which literally means "discharges"). These impromptu sessions attracted record companies from all over the world and are considered by many to be the precursor to the style of music that would later be known as *salsa* in New York. Some of these sessions were immortalized on classic recordings led by Israel "Cachao" López.

Aside from the night clubs, casinos, and café jams, radio was an important factor in the rise of Cuban music. It helped launch and sustain the careers of many titanic figures such as Arsenio Rodríguez, Isolina Carrillo, Orquesta Sensación, and Compay Segundo, who would later gain international stardom as the face of the Buena Vista Social Club.

AFRICAN INFLUENCE

Like most of the Caribbean and South America, Cuban culture is a mixture of indigenous, colonial (in this case, Spanish), and African influences. In Cuba, probably more so than anywhere else in the colonized world, the ties to traditional African religions and rituals remains strong even to this day. Nowhere is this more evident than in the music. When looking for the origins of Cuban music, we must start with the ritual music of the slaves who were brought to Cuba and the dances and song forms of the Spanish colonialists who brought them there.

There were three major *naciónes* (nations) of slaves brought to Cuba before slavery was abolished in 1887. There were the *Lucumi* (Yoruba) who came from western Nigeria, eastern Benin, and Ketu; the *Congo* (Bantu) who came from Burundi, Rwanda, and Namibia; and the *Calabaris* (Calabar) who were taken from Cameroon and the Lake Chad region. The people of each nación brought with them their own unique religions, rituals, and rhythms.

The different naciónes were often split up and spread out across the country in an effort to erase any connection to their origins. One of the ways that the slaves were able to maintain their identity was to gather to "beat the drum" when the plantation owners weren't looking or felt generous enough to allow it as a reward for hard work. As a result, many songs, dances, and rhythms found a home in the new world. Despite the efforts of many of the slave owners to rid the slaves of their African culture, the continued arrival of new slaves assured the connection to their origins was maintained. Rhythms, dances, and rituals were one way in which the slaves were able to do this.

Towards the end of slavery in Cuba, the various naciónes maintained their identities by sticking together in the cities and forming organizations known as *cabildos*. The cabildos were also a way for the government to keep tabs on the various former slaves. When slavery was eventually abolished in 1887, the cabildos were outlawed, and the different slave groups, who until then had been able to hold on to their identities, were assimilated into the greater society. The various cabildos were often forced to align themselves with the Catholic Church under the guidance of a patron saint.

From this point on, all that was left were the worship rituals, religious practices, and languages that defined the African identity in Cuban culture. These remaining cultural artifacts are preserved in the music.

Santería, or "The Way of the Saints," is a uniquely Afro-Cuban religion derived from the beliefs of the Yoruba people of Nigeria. Unable to openly worship the *orishas* of their native religion—orishas are spirits that manifest different aspects of the divine on Earth—they adopted Catholic saints as surrogates. By celebrating on the church-sanctioned saint's days, they were able to preserve many of their customs under the guise of Christianity. Santería's biggest influence on Cuban music was the importance of rhythm and dance. Many African religious ceremonies use sacred drumming as a means to communicate with the divine. The drummers play specific patterns for each orisha that combine to form complex, syncopated rhythms that are perfect for dancing. This is the root of the complex interplay of percussion instruments at the heart of Cuban music.

EUROPEAN INFLUENCE

If the African influence is responsible for the rhythmic content in Cuban music, the European (Spanish and, to a lesser extent, French) influence is responsible for the harmonic content and song forms. The music of Spain is itself a mixture of European, Arabic, Gypsy, Nordic, and Jewish influences, all of which made their way to Cuba.

With Catholicism being the main religion of the Spanish colonists, several Christian traditions survived the journey to the new world, such as the feast of the Epiphany and Corpus Christi. In Cuba, these became grand carnival celebrations, in which the cabildos were allowed to participate, in spite of the fact that they were still quite oppressed on every other level. It is during the parades of these festivals that the African influence and the Spanish influence came together in *comparsas* (groups of singers, dancers, and musicians that performed at carnivals).

Much like the carnival festivities of Brazil, each neighborhood and cabildo had its own comparsa. Each comparsa had its own unique flavor, evoking African deities with ritual masks, dances, and songs, while at the same time celebrating the harvest and seasonal changes that lead up to Lent. In modern times, each comparsa composes its own song and dance specifically for the procession. These processions are an expression of pride in one's neighborhood.

Cuba was also influenced by French culture, by way of New Orleans and especially Haiti (which was then known as Saint-Domingue). During the Haitian Revolution of the 1790s, many French colonists fled the country (sometimes bringing their slaves with them) and sought refuge in Cuba. The celebrations of the French slaves known as *tumba francesca* (or *tumba-francés*) were especially popular in the Oriente province. Much like the cabildos, tumba-francesca societies later became "freeman associations" when slavery was abolished. The tumba-francesca societies also participated in the Saint Day festivals performing a fast dance called the *cocoye*, which is based on a rhythm known as *cinquillo*. This rhythm later evolved into the *tumbao*, a rhythmic pattern that is the basis for the bass and conga in modern Afro-Cuban styles.

THE MIGRATION OF CUBAN MUSIC

It is important to realize that the music of Cuba and, for the most part, music in general during the Colonial era was primarily an accompaniment for dancing. The styles that exist today evolved from earlier versions that were based on European and African dances.

The *danzón*, which later evolved into the *mambo* and the *cha-cha-chá*, was based on the old English *contra dance*, which was adapted by the French and later transmitted to Cuba by way of Haiti. Over time, the *contradanza* (as it was known in Cuba) morphed into the less structured danzón in the Matanzas Province (see map on page 7).

While Havana is the capitol of Cuba, both politically and culturally, understanding the musical contributions of the rural regions of Cuba is essential. Most, if not all, of the classic styles of Afro-Cuban music were developed outside of Havana and brought there by the migration of those looking for a better life.

The *son* style grew out of several street song styles of Oriente (the eastern part of the country, encompassing provinces 11–15 on the map below) and is considered today to be the heart of Afro-Cuban music, more so than any other Cuban style. In Santiago de Cuba, the word "son" referred to all African styles of dance. The word later took on the meaning "festivity" in the western part of the island in and around Vueltabajo (a district in the Pinar del Río province). Since about 1920, the word "son" has encompassed not only the dances and the festive music but also the small bands that play it.

In 1909, a unique occurrence happened during President José Miguel Gómez's reign. Fearing that his army was conspiring against him, President Gómez ordered the company in Havana and the company in the Oriente to switch places. Several key son musicians including tres player Sergio Danger and guitarist Emiliano Difull were members of that Oriente company that was brought to Havana. According to legend, this was how the son made its way to Havana and, conversely, the guaguancó to Oriente.

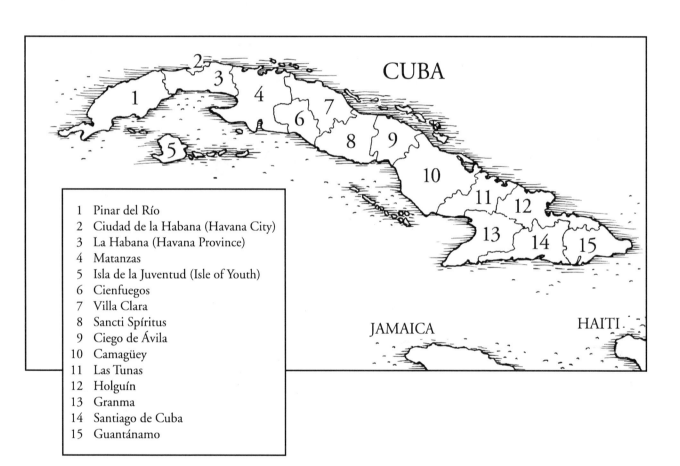

CUBA

1 Pinar del Río
2 Ciudad de la Habana (Havana City)
3 La Habana (Havana Province)
4 Matanzas
5 Isla de la Juventud (Isle of Youth)
6 Cienfuegos
7 Villa Clara
8 Sancti Spíritus
9 Ciego de Ávila
10 Camagüey
11 Las Tunas
12 Holguín
13 Granma
14 Santiago de Cuba
15 Guantánamo

JAMAICA

HAITI

THE GUITAR AND TRES IN CUBAN MUSIC

The guitar and its relatives hold a special place in Cuban music. Cuba was colonized by the Spanish, and the guitar plays a huge role in the music of Spain, so it only makes sense that the guitar would make its way into the roots of Cuban music. The guitar probably made its way to Cuba sometime in the fifteenth century. There were many different variations of the guitar including the *bandurria, vihuela, requinto,* and *laúd (or lute)*. They were primarily used as accompaniment to singing. Eventually, the guitar-like instruments evolved into the Cuban *tres*, which is the essential stringed instrument in Cuban music.

The tres traditionally has a smaller body than a regular guitar, although many *treseros* (tres players) prefer to convert a regular acoustic guitar. The tres has three sets of double strings, or *courses*. It was originally tuned to a D Minor chord (D–F–A), but since the revolutionary influence of Arsenio Rodríguez, the predominant tuning is a C Major chord (G–C–E) with the G and E strings tuned in octaves and the C strings tuned in unison.

Arsenio Rodríguez, who many consider to be the father of modern tres playing, was born in Matanzas Province in 1911, the grandson of slaves from the Congo. Not only did he revolutionize the way that the tres was played and tuned, but he also was a legendary band leader and composer who single-handedly changed the direction of Cuban music. Although he went blind at the age of seven, he began his professional career at the age of eight playing *botija* (see page 9) and *marimbula* (see page 11), both precursors to the bass. He soon took up the tres and rose to fame in the 1920s and 1930s, combining the tribal rhythms of *rumba* with the Spanish harmonies and melodies which made up the bulk of the repertoire for the guitar. Some of his most memorable gigs were with conga player Chano Pozo in a small group that featured piano, tres, and percussion.

Arsenio was an important figure in bringing the son style to Havana in the 1920s. At a time when most other son bands were downplaying their African influence, Arsenio was doing the opposite and changing the way that Cuban music was approached from a rhythmic standpoint. As well as changing the the rhythmic sound of the son and changing the way the instrument was tuned and played, he also changed the instrumentation that bands use. He expanded the lineup of the *septeto Habanero*, a group of seven musicians traditionally including strings, percussion, and a single trumpet. He added more trumpets, cowbell, and piano and opened up the form to include sections for improvised solos. By the late 1930s, he was bringing the *mambo* rhythm (based on a Congolese ritual pattern) into the mix, thus creating a whole new sound. The *conjunto* (big band) was the name given to the style that Arsenio had pioneered. This was the dawn of Cuban big band music.

Guitar (left); tres (right).

RHYTHM INSTRUMENTS

Bongos

Two small drums played between the knees. *Hembra* is the larger, "female" drum, and *macho* is the smaller, "male" drum. The bongos are usually responsible for accentuating and embellishing the rhythm.

Botija

A large clay jug originally used to carry water or olive oil. The player blows across the top of the jug to produce a bass note.

Cajón

A wooden box upon which the player sits. Typically found in rumba. Originally made by slaves out of wooden shipping crates.

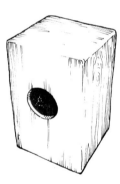

Claves

Two thick wooden sticks (one male, one female), which are struck together to create the clave rhythm. Possibly the most important rhythmic instrument in all of Cuban music.

Congas (Tumbadoras)

Barrel drums made from hardwood strips. Evolved from the *makuta* drums of Congo. Congas are grouped into three different sizes: *tumba* (large), *conga* (medium), and *quinto* (small).

Drumset

A set of drums consisting of kick (or bass) drum, snare drum, tom-toms, high-hat, and cymbals. Found in modern groups as well as Afro-Cuban jazz.

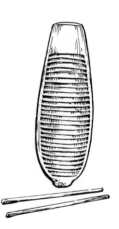

Güiro

A serrated calabash gourd that is scraped or hit with a stick or metal strip. Next to the clave, the güiro is one of the most important instruments in the rhythm section because it is responsible for keeping the pulse. It is typically the only instrument which keeps a steady downbeat.

Maracas (Rumba Shakers)

Dried calabash or gourd shells filled with seeds, often played in pairs. It is believed that maracas came from ancient Morocco. Maracas are deceptively hard to play, in that the instrument relies on a delayed response. Once shaken, the seeds must travel inside the gourd to hit the other side. As a result, the player must anticipate the rhythm.

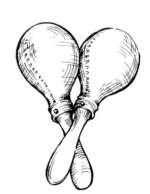

Marimbula

A wooden box fitted with metal prongs, like a larger version of the African *kalimba* or thumb piano. The player plucks the metal prongs to produce a percussive bass sound.

Shekeré

A large gourd covered in a mesh of beads or tiny shells. Brought to Cuba by the Yoruba, the instrument is shaken and hit with the palm of the hand for accents.

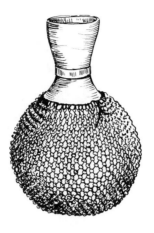

Timbales

Two mounted metal drums used for rhythmic embellishment and marking sections of a song. They are typically played with thin sticks striking both the shell and head of the drum.

TYPES OF CUBAN GROUPS

The Trio

As its name implies, a trio is a group of three singers who accompany themselves on guitar and small percussion instruments. The classic lineup consists of two singers playing guitar while the third played maracas. Sometimes, all three play guitars, and other times one plays tres or even clave. The trio is Cuba's version of the European *troubadour* or wandering minstrel tradition. It rose to prominence in the 1920s interpreting the bolero, guaracha, and son.

The Sexteto

The *sexteto* is the classic lineup of the son style, as Arsenio Rodríguez's "Sexteto Habanero," one of the first sextetos, demonstrated. The instrumentation consists of guitar, tres, bass, bongo, maracas, and clave. This type of collective came into existence in the 1920s.

The Septeto

As one would imagine, the *septeto*, which would go on to become the most important of Cuban bands, is a sexteto with the addition of a trumpet player. The most important of the septetos was Ignacio Piñeiro's Septeto Nacional, which started as a sexteto before adding a trumpet player in 1927.

The Conjunto

Further expanding of the traditional ensemble lineups continued into the 1940s when two or three trumpets as well as strings, vocalists, and a piano were added to the septeto. The final addition was the conga, first added to the conjunto by Arsenio Rodríguez. Today the conga is heard in almost all Cuban music.

The Combo

The combo is Cuba's version of a modern jazz group. There are no set lineups, but the traditional combination of trumpet, saxophone, bass, piano, and drumset is the template around which this type of group is based. There are versions that include electric guitar and tres as well. Again, like its American jazz counterpart, the combo is a reduction of a big band in order to fit into smaller venues and save costs when touring.

Chapter 2 LATIN RHYTHMS

CUBA

Havana

CLAVE

The *clave* is not only the name of an instrument, but it is also the name of the rhythm it plays. The clave is the underlying rhythmic pulse of all Cuban music. It is a simple, yet deceptive two-measure rhythmic figure of African origin that provides a constant point of reference for each instrument. If you were to look at the complex rhythms of the various styles of Cuban music as a house, the clave would be the foundation upon which every instrument and part stands.

Not only is the clave the rhythmic point of reference for all of the other instruments, but each of the other instruments plays a highly syncopated part relative to the clave that all add up to create the quilt of Cuban music.

2/3 Clave

There are several different variations of the clave. The most common is the *2/3 clave*. The name simply refers to the fact that there are two attacks in the first measure and three in the second measure. In the chart below, the numbers refer to the downbeats, and the "&" symbols the upbeats.

1	&	2	&	3	&	4	&	1	&	2	&	3	&	4	&
		x		x				x				x			x

3/2 Clave

The clave is also played in the reverse order; this is known as the *3/2 clave*. It is essential for each player to realize which clave is being played for each different style. When the wrong clave is played, the rhythm becomes *cruzado* or crossed.

1	&	2	&	3	&	4	&	1	&	2	&	3	&	4	&
x			x			x			x		x				

Guaguancó Clave

Certain rhythmic styles such as the *guaguancó* (which will be discussed at length in Chapter 4) have their own clave. It is also sometimes known as the *rumba clave*.

1	&	2	&	3	&	4	&	1	&	2	&	3	&	4	&
x			x				x			x		x			

Columbia Clave

In many Cuban rhythmic styles there are two separate rhythmic undercurrents happening simultaneously. One is in $\frac{4}{4}$ and the other is based on groups of 3, 6, or 12. As a result, there are several claves where the rhythm in groups of three is dominant. The most common is the *columbia clave*.

1	2	3	4	5	6	1	2	3	4	5	6
x		x			x		x		x		

Combining Columbia and Guaguancó Claves

Notice how the columbia and guaguancó claves are approximately the same pattern, even though they are in different time signatures. These two undercurrents are present in many Afro-Cuban rhythms.

Columbia Clave	1	2	3	4	5	6	1	2	3	4	5	6
	x		x			x		x		x		
Guaguancó Clave	x			x			x		x		x		
	1	&	2	&	3	&	4	&	1	&	2	&	3	&	4	&

When seen in this light, it is easy to see how important a good relationship with the clave is. Rhythms are simply divisions of time. It's like evenly folding a piece of paper in half, quarters, thirds, or whatever number you want. The piece of paper is still the same size. Likewise, a beat or measure is always the same size. The ways in which to divide it are many. In Cuban music, there are two pieces of paper, one divided into quarters and one into thirds (both rhythms happening simultaneously); it's the clave that shows us how to line the pieces of paper up.

CASCARA

Cascara is a two-measure rhythmic pattern that interlocks with the clave. Sometimes, the actual claves (the instruments) will be absent, but the clave rhythm is still implied by the cascara. The word cascara literally means "rind" or "shell." It refers to the outside part of the drum where the rhythm is usually played. It's played either on the side of the conga or the side of the timbales with a wooden stick or sometimes on a woodblock.

Cascara for 2/3 Clave

Count	1	&	2	&	3	&	4	&	1	&	2	&	3	&	4	&
Cascara	x		x		x	x		x	x		x	x		x		x

Cascara with Clave

Notice how the cascara and the clave line up.

Count	1	&	2	&	3	&	4	&	1	&	2	&	3	&	4	&
Cascara	x		x		x	x		x	x		x	x		x		x
Clave			x		x				x				x		x	

The cascara for the 3/2 clave would simply be the opposite of the 2/3.

TUMBAO

A defining feature of Afro-Cuban music is its extensive use of *syncopation*. Rather than emphasize the downbeats, syncopated music emphasizes the upbeats or "ands" (&). We see this in the clave and the cascara and how they relate to each other. The avoidance of beat 1 by the bass is an essential part of the Cuban feel. Before there was bass in Cuban music, the lower register was played by the botija, a large clay jug that was used to transport olive oil from Spain. As you can imagine, the number of pitches that could be played were quite limited. This is the main reason why the harmonic/melodic content of an Afro-Cuban bass line is fairly simple, for the most part using only roots and 5ths. However, what these bass parts lack in melody, they make up for in rhythm.

The rhythmic pattern played by the bass is known as *tumbao*. Tumbao is a one- or two-bar figure that accents the "and" of beat 2 and beat 4. The *ponche* is the fourth beat of the measure on the "3 side" of the clave. This beat is extremely important because the bassline/harmony shifts on beat 4 as opposed to beat 1. The ponche is often tied to the first beat of the "2 side" of the clave, so once the rhythm is set in motion, in essence, all one hears is the "and" of 2 and beat 4.

Tumbao with Clave

Ponche

Count	1	&	2	&	3	&	4	&	1	&	2	&	3	&	4	&
Clave			x		x				x			x			x	
Tumbao				x			x					x			x	

Tumbao

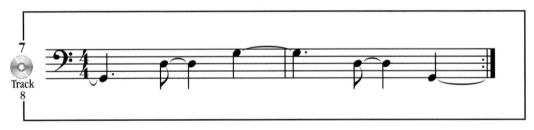

7

Track 8

Tumbao Conga Pattern

The basic conga pattern is also a variation of the tumbao. The different conga strikes are notated P = Palm, T = Tip, S = Slap, O = Open High, and LO = Open Low.

Count	1	&	2	&	3	&	4	&	1	&	2	&	3	&	4	&
Palm	x						x		x							
Tip		x		x		x				x				x		
Slap			x								x					
Open High							O	O							O	O
Open Low											LO	LO				

P T S T P T O O   P T S LO LO T O O

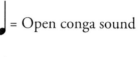

♩ = Open conga sound

✗ = Muted conga sound

Complete 2/3 Pattern

The following example is the complete rhythmic accompaniment for the 2/3 clave and a summary of the different rhythmic patterns that we've explored so far.

Count	1	&	2	&	3	&	4	&	1	&	2	&	3	&	4	&
Clave			x		x				x			x			x	
Cascara	x		x		x	x		x	x		x	x		x		x
Bass Tumbao				x			x					x			x	
Conga Tumbao	P		T	S	T	P		T	O	O	P	T	S	LO	LO	T	O	O

P T S T P T O O   P T S LO LO T O O

Chapter 3 GUAJEO/MONTUNO

Havana ★ CUBA

One of the key characteristics that sets Cuban music apart from many other types of music is the unique relationship between the fundamental elements of music: rhythm, melody, and harmony. In the music of Cuba, all three elements play an equal role in how the music sounds. Not only that, but each of the elements is highly developed.

The rhythms, as we learned in Chapter 2, are syncopated and quite challenging to master. As we will learn in this chapter, the harmonic content can be quite sophisticated, and the way in which the harmony is played—using arpeggios for a melodic effect—is also challenging.

The melodic manifestation of harmony in Cuban music, when played with the various syncopations, is known as *guajeo* or *montuno*. These two words have somewhat similar meanings, but in general, guajeo is played by a string instrument and montuno by the piano. Although they are often interchangeable, we will use the term guajeo in this book. The guajeo is the repeated melodic phrase or *vamp* that outlines the harmony.

Melodically and harmonically speaking, the music of Cuba is based on triads and 7th chords. Since 7th chords are in essence a combination of two triads, realizing how to play the triads in a melodic fashion over the complete fretboard is an essential skill to playing the guajeos that make up the bulk of the repertoire for the guitar and tres in Cuban music.

The following exercises and diagrams are designed to get you familiar with all of the triadic possibilities—both major and minor—as well as the dominant 7th chord possibilities across the entire fretboard.

CHORD THEORY REVIEW

A *chord* consists of three or more notes played simultaneously to create harmony. A *triad* is a three-note chord. All of the triads in this book are either major or minor. A major triad is constructed using the formula 1–3–5. The 1 or *root* is the note that gives the chord its name (for example, the root of a G Major chord is the note G). The next note is an interval of a major 3rd above the root. The final note is a perfect 5th above the root. For example, a G Major triad is spelled G–B–D.

Minor triads use the formula 1–♭3–5. They have a minor, or flatted, 3rd, which gives them their distinct sound. A G Minor triad is spelled G–B♭–D.

A *dominant 7th chord* has the formula 1–3–5–♭7. It is a major triad plus an extra note a minor 7th above the root. Dominant chords have a tense sound that wants to resolve back to the I chord. A G7 chord is spelled G–B–D–F.

Roman Numerals
When analyzing chord progressions, it is customary to assign each chord or triad a Roman numeral, indicating which scale degree of the key is the root of the chord. Upper-case numerals represent major chords, and lower-case numerals represent minor chords. For example, in the key of G Major, I stands for a G Major triad, ii is an A Minor triad, iii is a B Minor triad, and so forth. V7 indicates a dominant 7th chord built on the 5th scale degree (D7 in the key of G).

Roman Numerals
I or i................ 1
II or ii............. 2
III or iii........... 3
IV or iv............ 4
V or v.............. 5
VI or vi........... 6
VII or vii........ 7

LINKING GUAJEO WITH THE CLAVE

The trick to executing the guajeos correctly is knowing how to link them with the correct clave and cascara. There are a few "telling beats" that indicate which clave is being used and serve as the connection point where the guajeo pattern rhythmically locks into the clave pattern. As with all other aspects of clave, linking the melodic pattern correctly to the rhythm is essential, otherwise the rhythm becomes cruzado (crossed). If this happens, the groove sounds awkward and is uncomfortable to dance to. Cuban musicians treat their relationship with the clave with great pride. A musician who is cruzado will soon be out of a job.

The following examples are meant to show you the rhythmic linking points to the various claves. Listen carefully until you can really hear the subtle differences of each.

The strongest two beats in either the 2/3 or 3/2 clave are beat 2 of the "2 side" and beat 4 of the "3 side."

Or, in other words, beat two of the first measure of the 2/3 or second measure of the 3/2 and beat four of the second measure of the 2/3 or the first measure of the 3/2.

Strong Beats of the 2/3 Clave

Count	1	&	2	&	3	&	4	&	1	&	2	&	3	&	4	&
Strong Beats			x												x	
2/3 Clave			x		x				x			x			x	

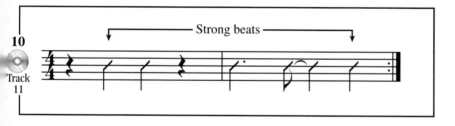

Strong Beats of the 3/2 Clave

Count	1	&	2	&	3	&	4	&	1	&	2	&	3	&	4	&
Strong Beats							x				x					
3/2 Clave	x				x		x				x		x			

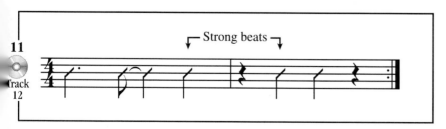

Son Montuno

The example below shows a typical guajeo that emphasizes the strong beats. Notice that the guajeo does not line up note-for-note with the clave, but rather dances around it to create a complex rhythmic pattern. Playing the accents on the strong beats will help you lock in with the clave.

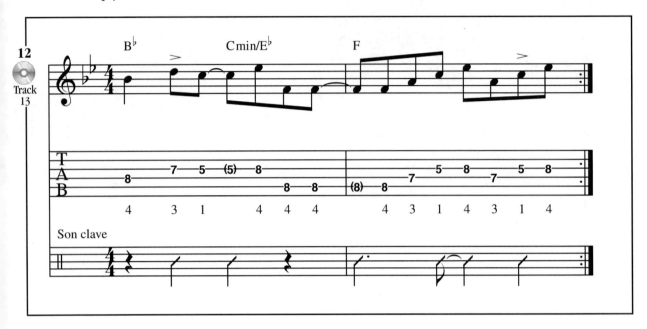

Against the Guaguancó Clave

Because the guaguancó clave is slightly different from the standard clave, it has slightly different strong beats. The accent on the "3 side" moves from beat 4 to the "and" of beat 4, as the following example illustrates.

TRIAD STUDIES

To gain the type of proficiency needed to express the complex rhythms discussed earlier, you must have a strong command of *triadic arpeggiation*, in other words, playing each note of the triad separately rather than strumming them all at the same time. The diagrams in this section show all of the possibilities on each group of three strings (EBG, BGD, GDA, and DAE). Limiting yourself to three strings at a time simulates the sound of the tres. Since most of the harmonic content of Cuban music is based on the I, IV, and V chords (either major or minor) of any given key, knowing how they relate is of chief importance. In the diagrams that follow, the I chord is always white, the IV chord black, and the V chord gray. The diagrams are in the key of G, but can be transposed to other keys by moving the shapes up or down the fretboard. The I–IV–V groups are shown separately, then together on one fretboard diagram.

○ = Tones in the I chord
● = Tones in the IV chord
◐ = Tones in the V chord

Major I–IV–V (G, B, and E Strings)

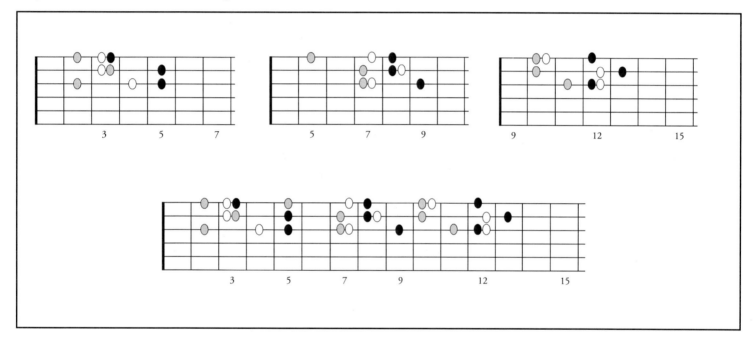

Now that you have spent time some exploring major I–IV–V triads on the E, B, and G strings, you're ready to apply the same concept to the remaining three-string sets.

Major I–IV–V (D, G, and B Strings)

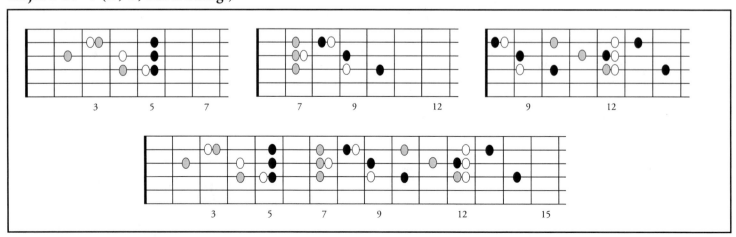

Major I–IV–V (A, D, and G Strings)

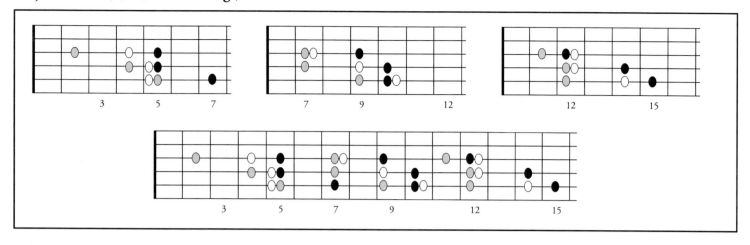

Major I–IV–V (E, A, and D Strings)

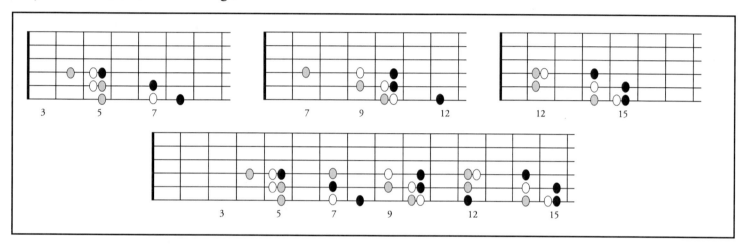

Just as important as the major I–IV–V progression is its minor counterpart, i–iv–V7. Both major and minor I–IV–V progressions are found in all of the various styles of Cuban music. These diagrams are in the key of G Minor, but can be transposed to any key. You may notice there are more gray dots; that is because the V7 arpeggio consists of four notes instead of three. Also, certain notes have been doubled so you can play them wherever they best fit the music.

Minor i–iv–V7 (G, B, and E Strings)

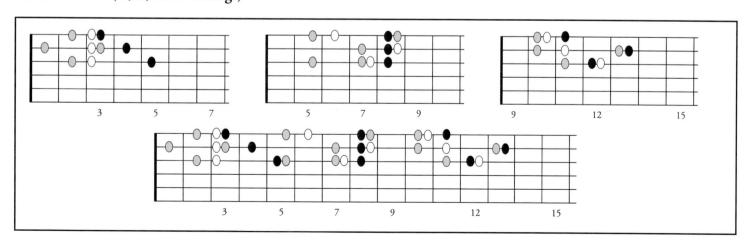

The following exercise is a i–iv–V7 progression in G Minor based on the 2/3 clave. It uses only the top three strings: E, B, and G. As already mentioned, Cuban music is highly syncopated. Often, with syncopation there also comes a *staccato* feel (notes played in a short, detached way); listen to "Agua con Gas" on the CD for a demonstration of this.

AGUA CON GAS
Track 16

Now that you've spent some time on the minor i–iv–V7 progression on the E, B, and G strings, let's apply the same concept to the remaining three-string sets.

Minor i–iv–V7 (D, G, and B Strings)

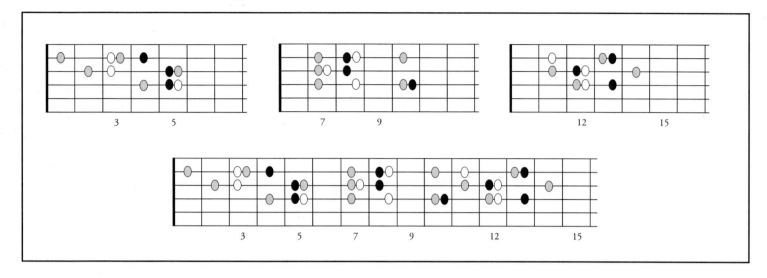

Minor i–iv–V7 (A, D, and G Strings)

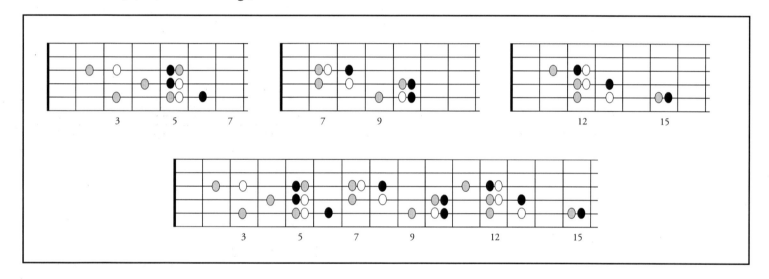

Minor i–iv–V7 (E, A, and D Strings)

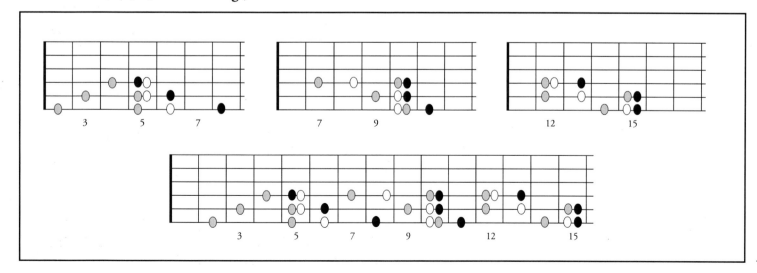

While I–IV–V progressions are a good place to start when learning to play guajeos, there are many other chord progressions you will come across when playing Afro-Cuban music. The following examples demonstrate a few of the more common progressions.

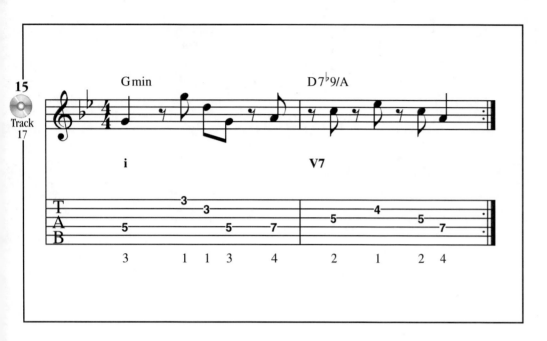

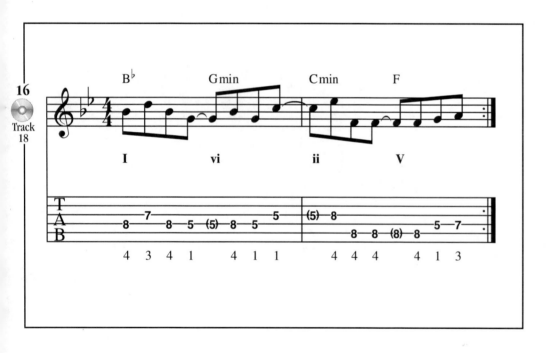

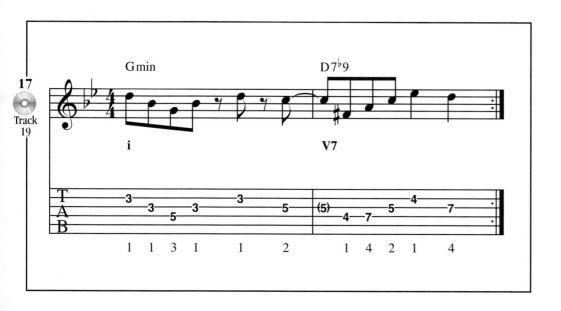

The following example is easiest to play using the fingerstyle technique.

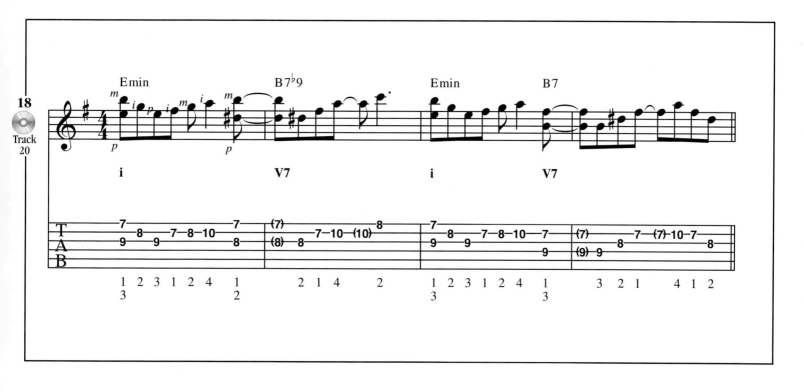

RHYTHMIC BREAKS

We have learned in this chapter that the melodic and harmonic element of Cuban music is quite unique. That being said, the main appeal of Afro-Cuban music for most people is its incredible rhythms. In some styles, such as the descarga (jam session), the entire song can be based on one continuous two-chord progression. One way to create distinct sections in a tune where the chord progression is the same throughout is to insert little breaks between sections. There exists a common set of rhythmic/melodic figures that are used to mark sections, or to separate an instrumental solo from the *coro* (part of the tune where everyone sings the main theme) and the coro from the montuno section.

The next few examples show some of the more common breaks.

Following is a descending arpeggio ending on the ponche in the 3 side of a 2/3 clave.

Count	1	&	2	&	3	&	4	&	1	&	2	&	3	&	4	&
Clave			x		x				x				x		x	
Break	x								x	x	x	x	x	x		

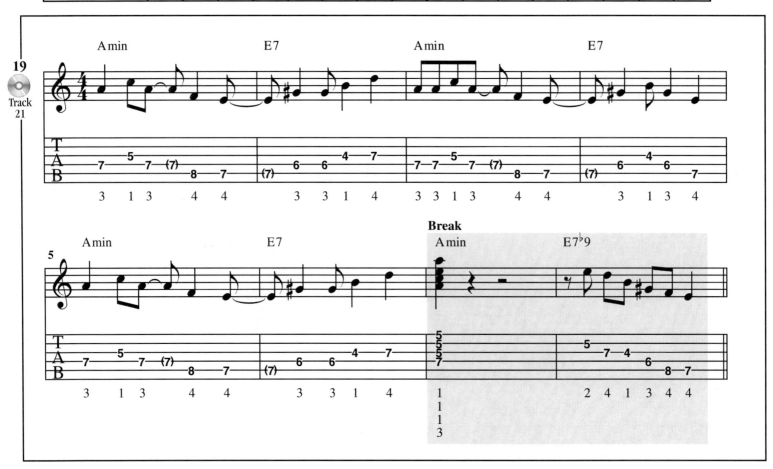

Next is an ascending arpeggio based on the 3/2 clave.

Count	1	&	2	&	3	&	4	&	1	&	2	&	3	&	4	&
Clave	x				x				x				x		x	
Break	x	x			x			x	x			x	x	x	x	

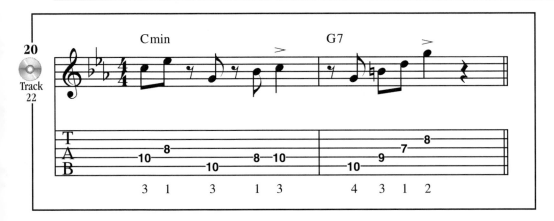

Finally, here is a rhythmic break that utilizes eighth notes and eighth-note triplets based on the 2/3 clave. Eighth-note triplets are one third of a beat in duration and are counted "1-trip-let, 2-trip-let, 3-trip-let, 4-trip-let."

Count	1	trip	let	2	trip	let	3	trip	let	4	trip	let	1	trip	let	2	&	3	&	4	&
Clave				x			x						x				x			x	
Break	x		x	x		x	x	x	x	x	x	x	x		x	x				x	x

Chapter 4
STYLES

CUBA

SON

The son emerged in Cuba around 1900 as an urban, popular dance-music style. It derived some features from Spanish music, including its harmonies and the use of the guitar and tres. To these, it added characteristics of the rumba. Features derived from the rumba include the clave rhythm and a two-part formal structure. This structure consists of a songlike first section followed by a longer second section featuring call-and-response vocals and instrumental improvisations over a repeated chordal pattern. By the 1940s, the son had become the most popular dance music in Cuba, Puerto Rico, and much of urban Africa; Puerto Ricans who moved to New York City brought the son with them. In the early twentieth century, son was a loose term which encompassed most of the rural music, much like the rural blues of the United States. By the 1920s, however, the standard configuration of son musicians was a septeto comprised of trumpet, guitar, tres, bass (or marímbula), bongos, maraca, and claves.

The son is characterized by the highly syncopated nature of its groove. None of the musicians accent the first beat of the measure.

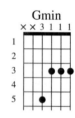

The son begins with the statement of the theme followed by a break and then the montuno, which opens up the song for soloing. Usually the sections are punctuated by *mambos*, unison breaks played by the rhythm section. In the following tune, most of the guitar part can be played by forming chords with the left hand. For example, the entire intro can be played by keeping your left hand in the form of the Gmin chord shown to the right.

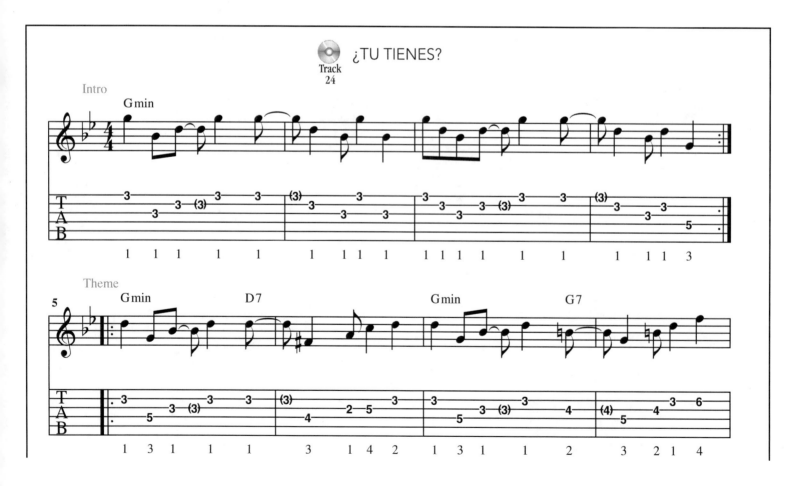

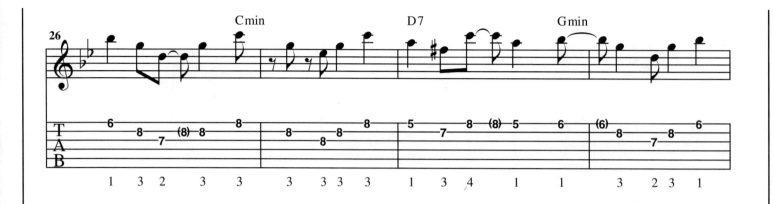

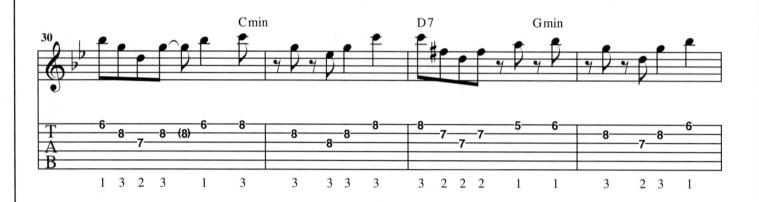

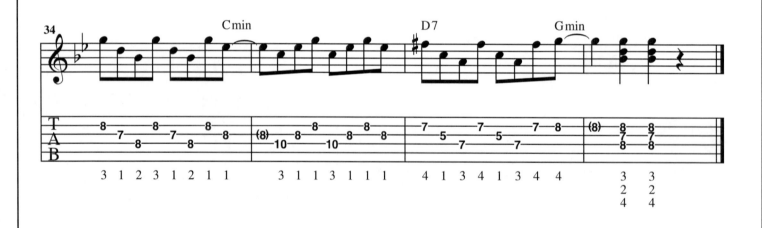

SON MONTUNO/GUAJIRA

Son montuno is a slower son influenced by the *guajira* (a style of rural song with Spanish origins that utilizes guitars and bongos). Usually, a simple I–IV–V chord progression is the vehicle for improvisation.

HOMBRE CALVO

Track 25

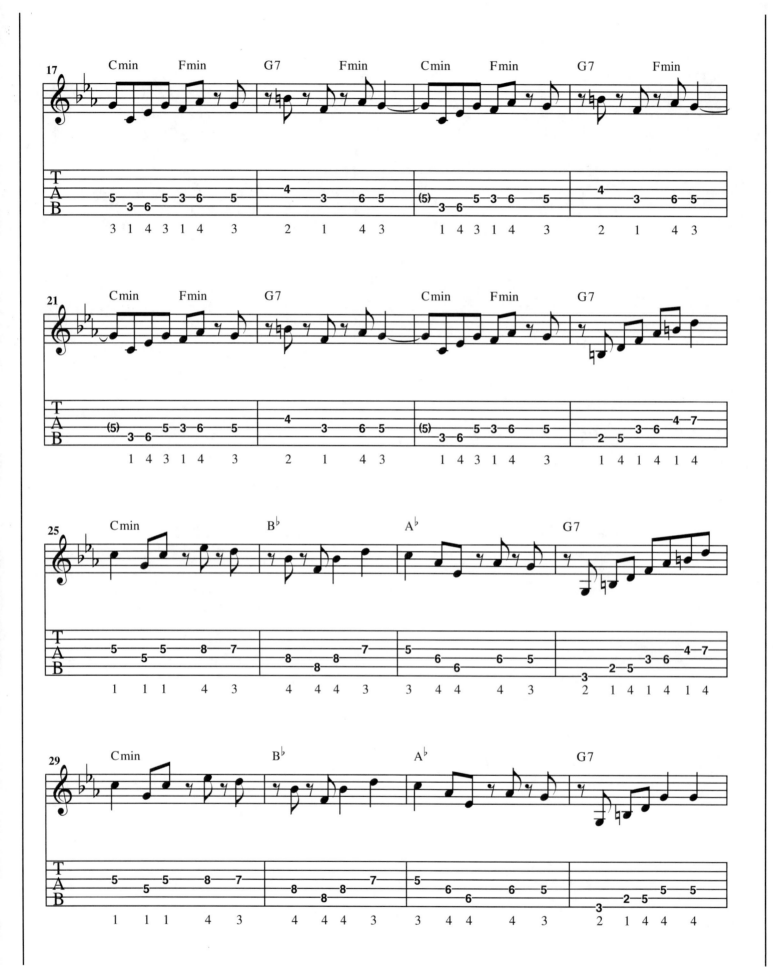

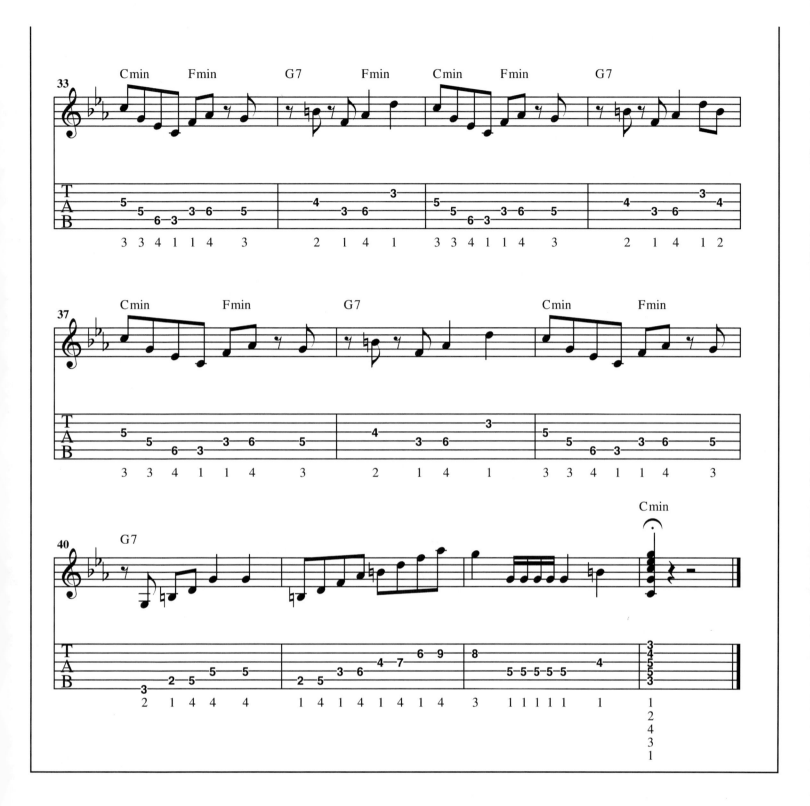

CHANGÜÍ

Changüí originated in the mid-nineteenth century in the rural areas around Guantánamo. The changüí is a highly syncopated style that is believed to have been a major influence on the son.

CHEENA MORENA

Track 26

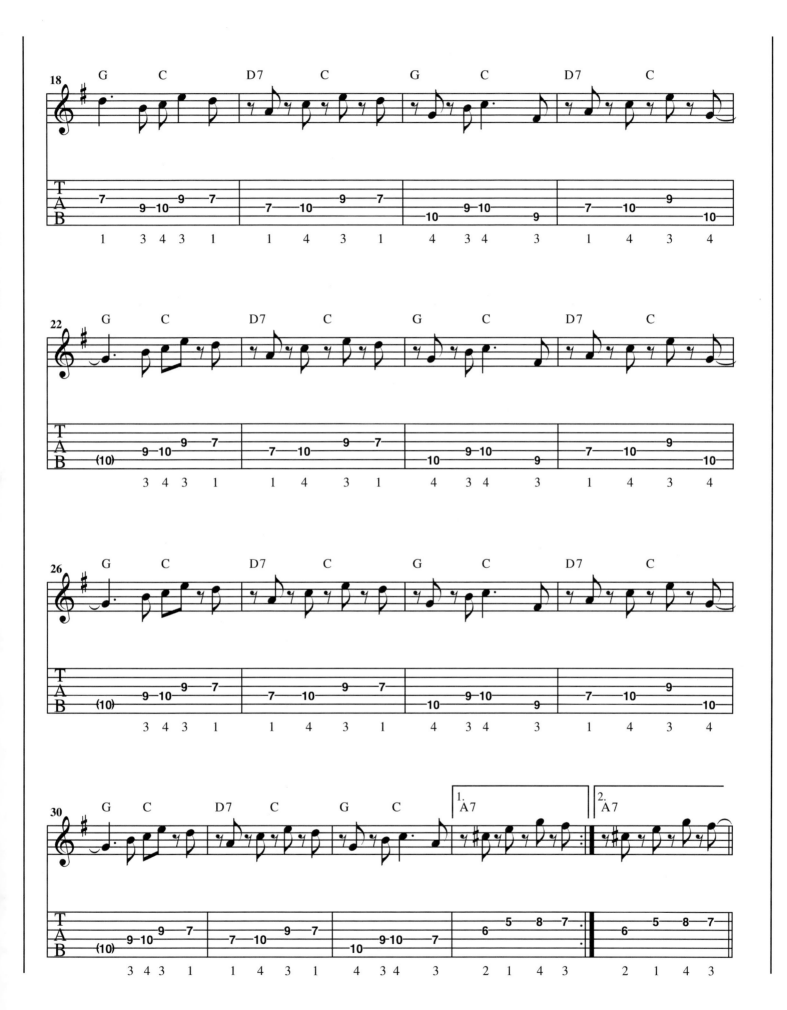

BOLERO

Bolero is a slow, romantic song style that is rooted in old Spanish dances. It arrived in Oriente around 1810. One of the first true Cuban boleros was "Tristeza," written in 1885 by Pepe Sánchez. The guitar is a prevalent instrument in bolero, usually used to accompany the singer. A semi-percussive strumming style known as *rayado* is utilized by bolero guitarists.

LAS GUAJIRAS DEL INVERNADERO

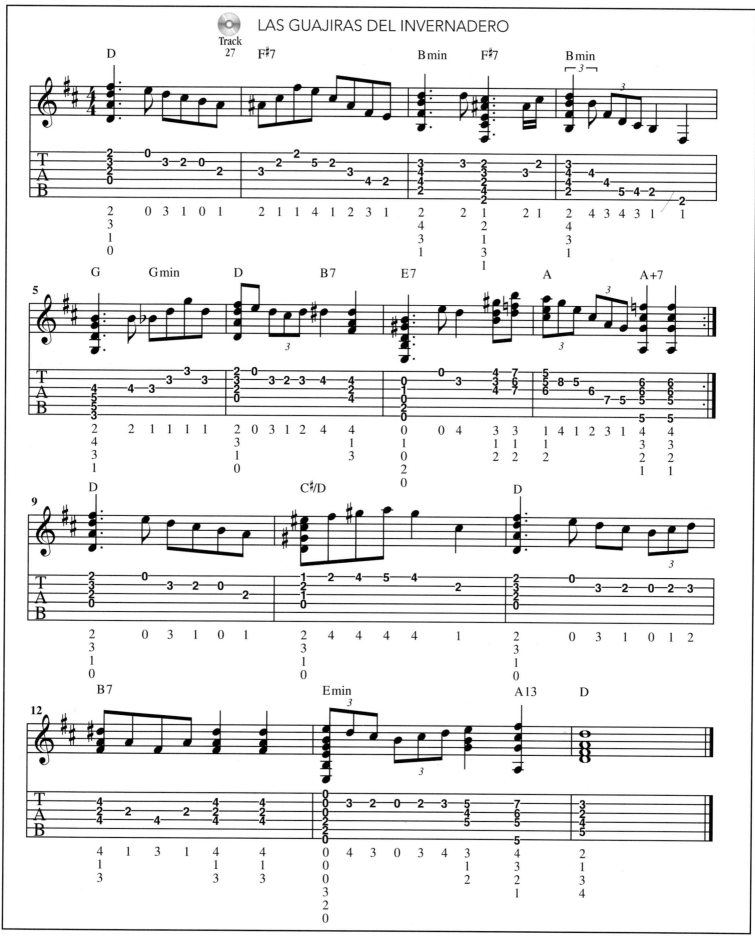

NUEVA TROVA

The term *trova* originally referred to a singer/guitar player from Oriente. The musical style
of *nueva trova* emerged in the 1960s and can be considered Cuba's political folk music, as
the lyrics often contain satirical evaluations of the government as well as social commentary.
The style is defined by its flowing $\frac{6}{8}$ rhythm. This song uses the fingerstyle technique.

LA PROXIMA

Track 28

DANZÓN

Danzón is derived from early nineteenth century French contradanzas and European ballroom dances and was originally written to accompany similar dances for the upper classes of Cuba. Its strong rhythmic undercurrent lead to the evolution of the cha-cha-chá and the mambo.

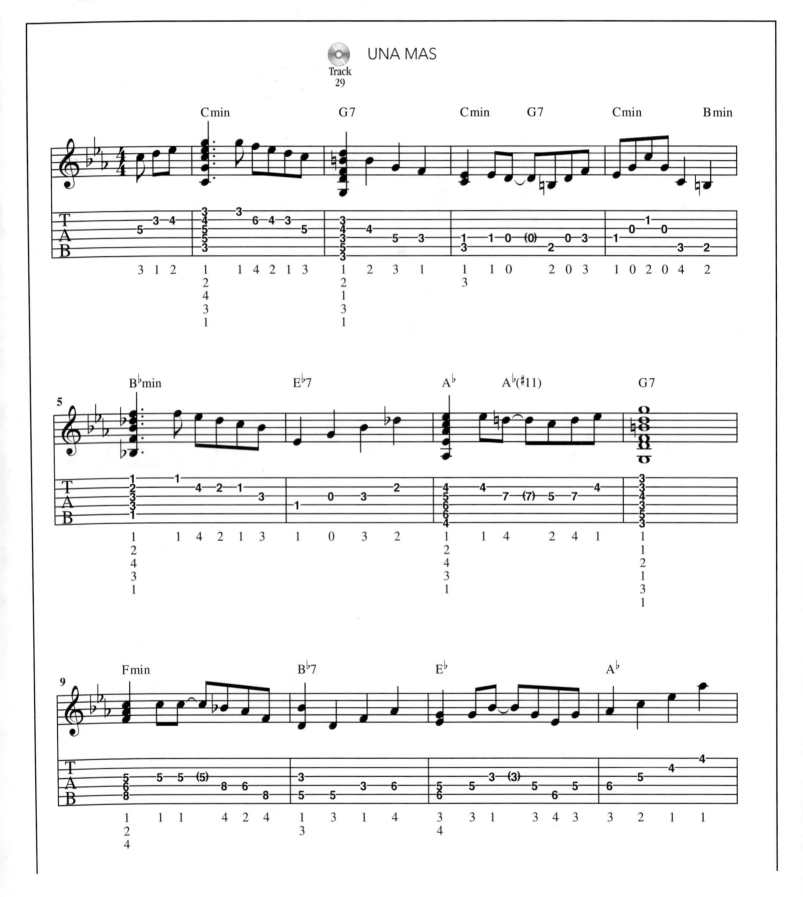

UNA MAS

Track 29

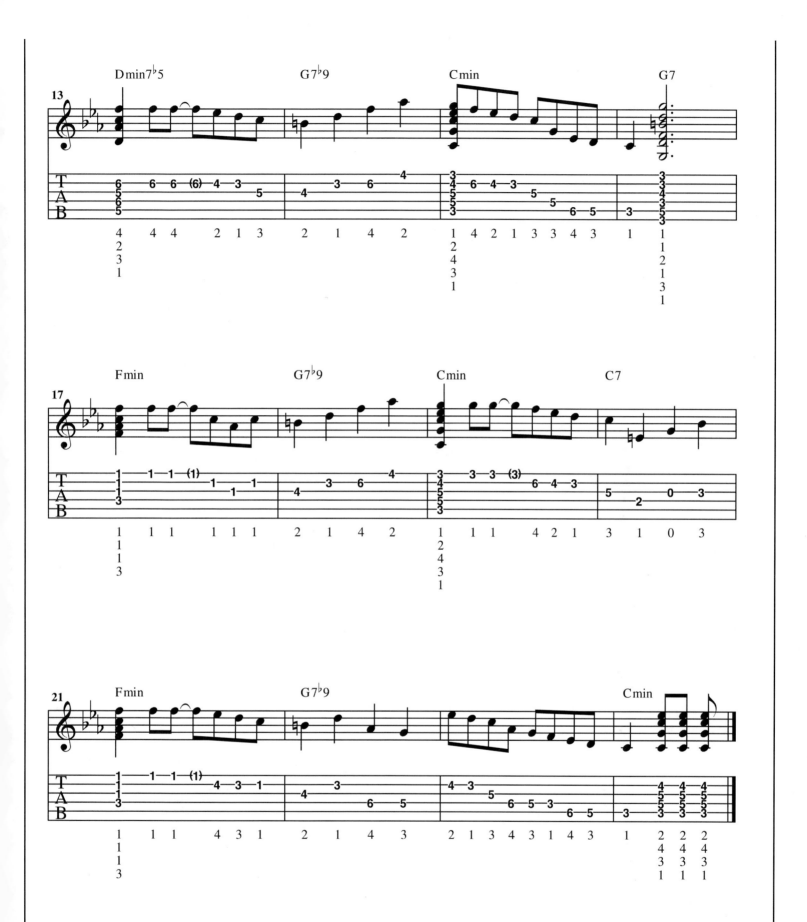

43

MAMBO

The *mambo* came to prominence in the early 1950s. Pérez Prado is almost single-handedly responsible for putting the style on the map. The mambo is first and foremost a dance music, created as a backdrop for ballroom dancing events. It is normally performed by a big band, and notable singers include Benny Moré, Celia Cruz, and Daniel Santos. The following example can be played either fingerstyle or with the pick.

BLUE BRITO

Track 30

GUAGUANCÓ

The guaguancó is a type of rumba characterized by the highly syncopated rhythms based on the guaguancó clave. This style is also very connected to the spiritual and religious Santería dances found in the countryside.

ARROZ CON POLLO

FINAL WORD

This concludes *Guitar Atlas: Cuba.* The next step is to listen to as much Cuban music as you can, both recorded and live (if possible). Cuban music is all about rhythm and feel, qualities that are best developed through listening and practice. Good luck!